The Little Book of The Sales Questions You Wished You'd Asked

99 Insightful Questions for Every Sales Situation

The Art and Science of Asking Questions is the Source of all Knowledge
Thomas Berger

By Clive Howarth

Live, Love, Learn, Leave a Legacy
Stephen Covey - The 8th Habit

Copyright © 2019 by Clive Howarth. All Right Reserved.

No part of this publication may be reproduced, distributed, or transmitted in any form or by any means, including photocopying, recording, or other electronic or mechanical methods, or by any information storage and retrieval system without the prior written permission of the publisher, except in the case of very brief quotations embedded in critical reviews and certain other non-commercial uses permitted by copyright law. The rights of the author to be identified as the originator of this work have been asserted in accordance with the Copyright, Design and Patents Act 1988.

Preface - Why I wrote this book

I've spent over twenty-five years training professional sales forces to improve their performance and before that, I headed up IBM UK General Systems Division's sales training for a couple of years as well as being an IBM salesman and sales manager. I was exceptionally lucky because I worked for a company that invested in me and trained me properly. In fact, it took eighteen months to train as an IBM sales representative. But most of us aren't so fortunate and how many of us have that luxury today? Not many.

However, some of us do get some sales training. We go on a course or two. Maybe we do some online internet courses or read some books on selling. Some of us are thrown in at the deep end with little or no training and left to sink or swim and others are expected not only to do their own professional job, but also find and secure more business as well - maybe without any training at all.

Something I've noticed from my training courses, especially in a roleplay where we practise sales calls, is the inability of even confident and experienced salespeople to ask good, well-crafted questions. What's a 'good' question you may say? It's one that gives you precisely the information you are seeking.

This book is a compilation of many of the questions I know you want to ask in your pursuit of sales success. They are my words and my phrasing, and I hope they will give you a basis for planning your sales calls and feeling confident with your questioning.

Contents

Preface - Why I wrote this book	3
1. Introduction (*who should read this book*)	5
2. A bit on Questioning	6
3. How to ask Questions	8
4. What do you ask Questions about?	10
A. What is the effect of this problem on you and on the business?	12
B. How important, is the resolution of this problem to you and to the business?	13
C. What will it mean, to you and to the business in money terms, when this problem is resolved?	14
D. How do you make these kinds of decisions? What is the Decision Process?	15
E. What do you consider when you are making the decision? What are the Decision Criteria?	16
F. Who will make the decision? Who are the Decision Maker(s)?	17
G. Who else in the business will be affected?	18
H. How easy will it be to gain their support?	19
I. When do you want to do this?	20
J. How much do you expect to pay to resolve the problem?	21
K. What do they know about you and your company?	22
L. What is their impression of you and your company?	23
M. Who else are you talking to about solving this problem? Who are your Competitors?	24
N. How easy is it for you and for the business to accept change?	25
O. How might Internal Politics affect the sale?	26
Acknowledgements and Stuff	27

1. Introduction

come on, everyone can ask questions, can't they?

This book is for you if you if you find constructing questions difficult or you run out of ideas. It's also for you if you'd like to put a bit more variation in your questions, you know, when a customer wriggles out of an answer or doesn't give you the result you want. It's always handy to be able to re-phrase the question to enable you to dig a bit deeper.

Here's how to use the book

- Read it all the way through. It won't take long

- After you've planned your sales call and decided what your objectives are, look at the appropriate section of the book to see what questions might be useful

- Re-phrase them if you want, it's up to you

- Practise asking them before you meet your customer

2. A Bit on Questioning

it's a fundamental skill of every salesperson to be able to ask incisive, well-crafted, questions

You've done your planning, now you must put it into action.

Your ability to ask the right question at the right time is critical. You use questions to:

- **discover information** – *"How do you manage now?"*
- **to gain commitment** – *"Will you go ahead?"*
- **establish facts** – *"What are you thinking of spending on this?"*
- **determine opinions** – *"How are we doing?"*

Because, if you can't ask incisive questions you'll never find out what your customers really need. But, the best-constructed question will be useless unless its topic is relevant. So here are 15 essential topics and 99 insightful questions which you can use to plan, construct and deliver, to forward your sale.

You may have the best answer to your customers' problems but if you don't know how important this problem is to them or they don't believe you, they don't agree with you, can't afford you, they are not sure when they want to start, or the person to whom you are speaking hasn't the authority to place the order, you are wasting your time.

These questions are to help you 'qualify' your sales opportunity. To find out whether you have a realistic chance of getting the order; of winning the business; of closing the deal. And they'll give you some pointers as to what you must do to win the business. Because as I say in my book, The Little Book of Selling, chapter 10, *"It's pointless selling to people who can't buy or who can't influence the decision"*

So, think of your questions as surgical instruments with which to determine your customers' true wants, needs, intentions, and opinions. Used correctly they will uncover the route to your customer's satisfaction and to a sale. Used incorrectly and the waters will be muddied, and you will be lost.

3. How to ask questions

There are no set rules for this. You use the appropriate question at the right time. That's why you planned your sales call.

- Think about your question before opening your mouth
- Ask your question and <u>then shut up</u>. Give your customer time to answer
- Ask only one question at a time

Dangers of questioning

However, sometimes you and I are afraid of asking the question so we avoid it. If you are to be successful you must never, never, 'duck' a question. So here are the reasons and how to handle them.

You are afraid of looking foolish or ill-informed - simply admit you don't know, or didn't listen, or have forgotten and go ahead and ask the question

"I'm sorry, I know I should be aware of this. Please, will you remind me?"

You don't want to embarrass your customer - apologise and flag up that the question may be sensitive. Then ask it.

"This may seem intrusive, but to make sure I get the finances correct, I need to know your profit margins. What are they please?"

You are afraid of the answer - Simply have a plan for the what you will do if the answer is the one you fear most. For example, salespeople sometimes don't ask for the order because they fear rejection. Instead, they wait for the customer to place the order which sometimes never comes. A better plan is to think what you will do if the customer says "no". It's quite straightforward.

"That's disappointing. What have we missed?"

There is much more on this topic in my book The Little Book of Selling, chapter 8 – Essential Sales Skills

4. What do you ask questions about?

that's why you plan, isn't it?

Peter Thomson says you need to be able to answer these four questions when you are planning your sales calls.

- Why you?
- Why me?
- Why this
- Why now?

Here are 15 Topics which will help you answer these questions and others as well. I've assumed that your customer has a problem that you are seeking to help them resolve - they have PAIN in their organisation. But it may be an opportunity that you are planning to help them realise. There is a chance for GAIN. In this case, the questions will change slightly. Against each of the topics, I've suggested several questions from which to choose.

The topics are focused on the removal of, or solution to, a client's problem because this is the most common reason for a purchase - the removal of PAIN in a client's life or business. However, your client may want your help in seizing an opportunity – to access GAIN. In this case, the topics will need a little reframing. For example:

Instead of

    A. What is the effect of this problem on you and on the business?

Rephrase it to

    A. What will be the effect of realizing this opportunity for you and for the business?

The Topics

A. What is the effect of this problem on you and on the business?

B. How important is the resolution of this problem, to you and to the business?

C. What will it mean, to you and to the business, in money terms, when this problem is resolved?

D. How do you make these kinds of decisions? What is the Decision Process?

E. What do you consider when you are making the decision? What are the Decision Criteria?

F. Who will make the decision? Who are the Decision Maker(s)?

G. Who else in the business will be affected?

H. How easy will it be to gain their support?

I. When do you want to do this?

J. How much do you expect to pay to resolve the problem?

K. What do they know about you and your company?

L. What is their impression of you and your company?

M. Who else are you talking to about solving this problem? Who are your Competitors?

N. How easy is it for you and for the business to accept change?

O. How might internal politics affect the sale?

A. What is the effect of this problem on you and on the business?

It's important you find out exactly what this problem is doing to the business. What and where is the PAIN? Is it causing revenue loss? Is it creating complaints? Is it increasing stress? What is going wrong and who or what is being affected?

1. What impact does this situation have on the business?
2. What else is affected?
3. Have you any difficulties with...?
4. How does it affect...?
5. Where is it most noticed?
6. How does it impact your customers?
7. What effect does it have on your staff?
8. How are your suppliers affected?

"We cannot solve our problems with the same thinking we used when we created them"
Albert Einstein

B. How important, is the resolution of this problem to you and to the business?

So your customer has a problem, but does it matter, or is it something that they can manage? Is it going to get worse the longer it goes on? How much of the business is it affecting? Who knows about it? Who cares about it?

9. How important is it for you to improve ......?

10. What is the effect of this (situation) on….?

11. In an ideal world, what would you like to change? Why?

12. How long do you think this can go on for?

13. Who would benefit the most if you sorted this out?

14. Which part of the business is complaining most?

"The longer a problem goes on, usually, the worse it gets"

C. What will it mean, to you and to the business, in money terms, when this problem is resolved?

These questions are mainly about money. How much money will be saved? How much money will be made? But they may lead to other benefits too.

15. What are the key benefits you will derive from the change? What will they be worth?

16. What will it be worth to you to make the change?

17. How much will this save, this year; next year; over the length of the project?

18. How will you cost justify the solution?

19. How much more would you like to achieve?

20. How much would you like to see the situation improved?

"If you are not confident talking about money, bring along someone who is"

D. How do you make these kinds of decisions? What is the Decision Process?

All buying decisions follow some sort of process. Sometimes the process is very formal and involves tenders and presentations. Other times businesses and individuals buy on a whim. So, it is vitally important you find out what methods or processes, formal or informal, your customer uses to decide from whom to buy. How will they go about choosing a supplier?

21. How does your organisation normally set about purchases of this nature?

22. What steps do we need to take to progress this further?

23. Who else is involved?

24. What are the next moves?

25. How do we proceed from here?

"The risk of a wrong decision is preferable to the terror of indecision"
Maimonides

E. What do you consider when you are making the decision? What are the Decision Criteria?

What does you/your company have to
- **DO**
- **BE**
- **HAVE**

in order to win the business?

26. How do you select your suppliers?

27. What are you looking for from us? What else?

28. What are your key criteria for selection? What else?

29. What are your 'must haves'?

30. What are your 'nice to haves'?

31. What do you look for in a supplier? What else?

32. How, precisely will you decide?

33. How important is Price; Delivery; Reliability; Experience; Track-Record etc, etc?

34. What would your ideal supplier look like? What else?

F. Who will make the decision? Who are the Decision Maker(s)?

What are the names, titles and positions of the person or people who will make the final decision. How influential are, they? Who can say "no" when everyone else says "yes"?

35. Who else, apart from you will be involved?

36. What are their roles, their titles? Where do they fit in?

37. Who will you need to bounce these ideas off?

38. Who do you think is for this proposal? How influential are they?

39. Who do you feel might be against us? How influential are they?

40. How many copies of our proposal do you need? To whom should I address them?

41. Who can say "no" to this plan when everybody else says "yes"?

"Good decisions come from experience, and experience comes from bad decisions."

G. Who else in the business will be affected?

Often a decision taken in one department will impact other parts of the business. For example, a bank implements a new software system to improve security and all their customers have to change their passwords. The customers had no say in the decision but have been significantly affected by it. What other departments or parts of the business will be affected by this decision?

42. Which other people or departments will be affected by this?

43. Who do you think will notice the changes?

44. What about accounts; sales; your partners etc?

45. What do you think their reactions will be?

"A little Consideration, a little Thought for Others, makes all the difference"

A. A. Milne

H. How easy will it be to gain their support?

Other 'players' who are outside the formal process can informally influence a sale. You need to know who they are to make sure they understand the importance of your proposals and get them 'onside'. For example, the main decision maker's PA or secretary can often be very influential. The bank's customers weren't consulted, and some were not happy, but the bank explained the reasons and offered them a small credit. Only a few deserted.

46. Who do I need to talk to, to get them onside?

47. What's in it for them?

48. How do we 'sell' this to them?

49. How do we win them over?

50. What do we have to do to get their support?

51. If we can't convince them how do we work around them?

"Arouse in the other person an eager want. He who can do this has the whole world with him."
Dale Carnegie

I. When do they want to do this?

Sometimes customers invite you to bid but have no intention of placing business with you right now. They are doing some research for a future project. They need several quotations. Or they want to get a competitive quotation to pressurise their existing supplier. Or they want to establish a budget for the project. One way to uncover this is to ask for their timetable for the project.

52. When do you need our proposal by?

53. What's the planned start date?

54. When would you like to start?

55. How quickly will you decide?

56. How soon would you like to see the benefits?

57. How soon will you be ready to decide/implement?

58. What are your deadlines?

J. How much do you expect to pay to resolve the problem?

It's important that you know if your customer is prepared to pay you the right amount for the work you are proposing. Because if they haven't the money or their budget is not enough you won't make a sale. The Little Book of Selling Chapter 13 covers how to handle this.

59. How much are you planning to spend?

60. How much has been set aside?

61. What do you believe this will cost?

62. What is your budget for this?

63. How did you reach this figure?

64. Who controls this budget?

65. Are funds allocated for this? What are they?

66. Is this planned expenditure? What's the figure?

"Price is what you pay. Value is what you get."

Warren Buffett

K. What do they know about you and your company?

Customers may or may not know much about you. They may have been referred to you by one of your satisfied customers. They may have seen an advert or seen your name on Facebook, Twitter or LinkedIn. Maybe they looked you up on the Internet or responded to your marketing initiative. So, check them out and be prepared to tell them a bit about you and your company. The Little Book of Selling, chapter 18 will help here.

67. What do you know about us?

68. What have you heard about us?

69. Can I give you an update on……?

70. How much do you know about our products etc.?

71. How do you feel about our progress so far?

72. What are your views of/about……….?

73. How do you feel about what you have heard?

'It's a fine line between bragging and informing'

L. What is their impression of you and your company?

This is something you should check fairly frequently. If they already know you, be prepared to ask them what they think of both you (personally) and your company. If they don't know you, give them a bit of time and then start checking. Remember people buy from people. See The Little Book of Selling Chapter 14.

74. Am I making sense?

75. How do you feel about working with us?

76. What do you think of our people?

77. Are we the sort of people you can do business with?

78. Are you confident we can help you?

'First impressions are the most lasting'
Proverbs

M. Who else are you talking to about solving this problem? Who are your Competitors?

It's important to know who else they are considering because it's better to know your enemy than not. Of course, many companies won't tell you. It's also worth finding out if they already have a supplier and if so, why aren't they using them?

79. Who else are you considering for this project?

80. Have you looked at anyone else? Who?

81. Which other companies have you approached?

82. What experience have you in dealing with this type of….?

83. Who do you usually use for these matters?

84. Why aren't you using them for this one?

'I have been up against tough competition all my life. I wouldn't know how to get along without it'

Walt Disney

N. How easy is it for you and for the business to accept change?

Not many of us welcome change. We want everything to stay the same but get better. So, how will people react towards a new supplier; to a new procedure; to working a different way? How will other departments and customers accept change? It's important you know because many excellent projects have failed simply because they meant too much upheaval and too much change to the status quo.

85. How pleased are you with your present supplier?

86. How would you feel about considering an alternative?

87. In an ideal world, what more would you like?

88. What would stop you changing to another supplier, another process, a new building, a different advisor, etc?

89. What more can we do to secure your business?

'When in doubt, choose change'

Lily Leung

O. What about internal politics?

Many organisations have their own particular ethos and politics. Unless you are part of the organisation itself it's very hard to know how this works. But it's worth having a go at finding out if only to discover that you are unlikely to make a sale. I once lost a sale to a company in South Wales that made small parts for aircraft, and who really wanted my solution. But the holding company – a much larger supplier to the aircraft industry - had fallen out with their American partners so refused to do business with an American owned company. And I worked for IBM!

90. How do your management/staff feel about......?

91. What more are they looking for?

92. Who influences .... with their decisions?

93. How will the board react?

94. What do they want to happen?

95. How much does your manager know about .....?

96. How involved has your manager been with ......?

97. Does s/he know of our discussions?

98. What's their reaction?

99. Who will want to stop this? Why?

Acknowledgements and Stuff

This book is an accumulation of questions, that I have gleaned in over 25 years of working with salespeople. The people below, also have knowingly or in most cases unknowingly helped me. Just as I hope, that by writing this book, I may have helped you too. If you have, thanks for reading it.

Peter Thomson
Neil Rackham
Anita Woodcock
Carl Jung
Roger Reid
Sue Knight
Edward de Bono
Ken Blanchard
Fritjof Capra
W Timothy Gallwey
Sir John Whitmore
Openclipart
Nancy Kline

David Peoples
John Watson
Tony Robbins
David Merrill
Charles Handy
Stephen Covey
Tony Buzan
Chip and Dan Heath
Andrew Matthews
Sharon Drew Morgen
123RF Clipart
Brian Tracey
Barend ter Haar

Many of the above have shared their knowledge by writing books. Also, some have YouTube clips and websites. So, if you want to further your selling skills, I commend hitting the search engine of your choice and doing some research.

Watch out for further books planned, in this series.
- The Little Book of Selling – *A guide for aspiring salespeople*
- The Little Book of Opportunities - *How to find sales leads*
- The Little Book of Presenting - *How fearlessly, to deliver a compelling talk or presentation*
- The Little Book of Negotiating - *What you do when the customer says "yes I'm interested, but......"*

This book is for you if you need more sales but are spending too much time selling but not winning; if you love running your business but hate 'selling'; if the thought of asking for money terrifies you and if being rejected hurts. So, it's for you if you run your own business or if you are employed and have to find your own customers. It's also for professional salespeople to use as well. It is a reference book. It is a book you can learn from if you've not done any selling before. And it's a refresher book for you to re-read and remind yourself of good selling behaviours and techniques.

To buy it on Amazon use this link
                          myBook.to/LBSelling2

Just a thought

"If a person empties their purse into their head, no one can take it away from them - an investment in knowledge always pays the best interest."

Benjamin Franklin

Clive Howarth

Sales & Management Coaching

clivehowarth@gmail.com

Notes

Notes